For my beloved Father,

Miraz Sikder,

The Story of

MY SUPER-
DAD

ISBN: 978-1-3999-3262-2

www.nielsenbook.co.uk
Instagram: @lemon.plant

Author: Samira Sikder Illustrator: Samira Sikder

Want to know something cool?

Because I'm about to tell you a story about someone very special to me.

My DAD is actually a SUPERHERO!

I know it sounds crazy, but let me show you.

My Dad is like no other,
his superpowers are not
like those you see on TV
or in your comic books.

In fact, maybe your Dad has
the same superpowers too!

My Dad would help anyone in need. Even the smallest of birds that couldn't fly.

With my Dad's superpowers,

9

he would fix them back to
health so they could fly
back to their family.

My Dad could cook a meal for everyone. He could cook anything and everything you wanted. His food was the best!

His food was like
magic, people kept
coming back for
more!

My Dad could fix almost everything from broken bikes to our leaky sink and even my brother's toy car.

My Dad would take us on adventures in his Dadmobile.

We would go to faraway lands

and explore places we have
never been to before.

2010 Hook Light house
Co. Wexford

But then one day my Dad was taken to the hospital...

We were all very confused, we didn't know what was happening.

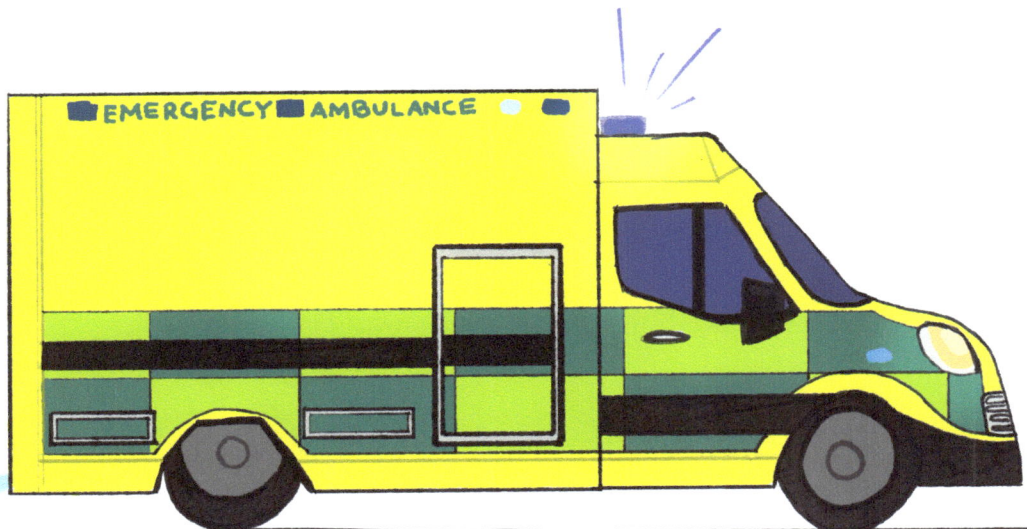

The doctor told us

'I'm afraid your Dad is sick but don't worry everything will be alright'.

We didn't understand what was happening but we knew as a family, we could get through anything together!

My Dad is different now. But that doesn't stop him from being a Super Dad.

We still go on adventures with his new Dadmobile!

My
Dad
can
always
make
us
laugh...

...and tell us stories.

My Dad can spend more time with us than ever before.

He has more time to play instead of working all day.

My Dad is always there for us when we get hurt. He puts plasters on our cuts and hugs us all better with his super hugs.

Even though he is different now, he is still my superhero. When I look at him, I see he's still the man he used to be. And no matter what happens, I'll always love my Super Dad.

About the Author/Illustrator

Hi, my name is Samira and I am a girl with a dream. I didn't write this in the third person because I wanted to talk to you, the people who are reading my little summer project. I have a dream to inspire and help others through my art. I made this book with love and poured my heart into the vivid colourful illustrations that I drew myself. This story is about my Dad with real events that actually took place in my life.

It can be hard losing someone you love to an illness especially when you are still very young. Though it might be hard seeing a completely new person who isn't like themselves anymore, you still remember the person they used to be. In my dad's case, he suffered from a brain stroke that caused him some memory loss and left him wheel-chair-bound. I wanted to commemorate my father's life and dedicate this book to him. He will always be someone I strive to be like and he will always be my superhero.

With this book, I wanted to reach out to other families and children who are going through a similar situation and tell them that they are not alone. This book is for love, hope and support. I want people to appreciate their loved ones and see the everyday little things they do that make them a superhero.

Also a huge thank you to the people who helped proof read and make this story even better. I couldn't have done it without you!

with love,

Samira

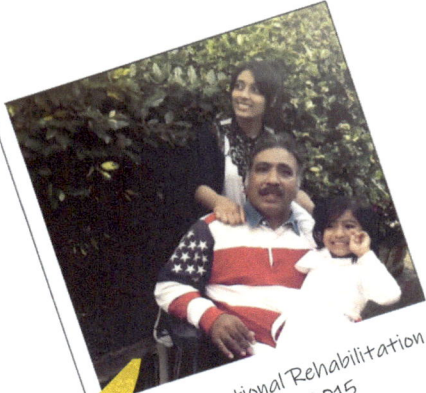

The National Rehabilitation
Centre, Dublin 2015

Family <3

ADVENTURES with my brother and dad!

First day of school

The Story of

MY SUPER DAD

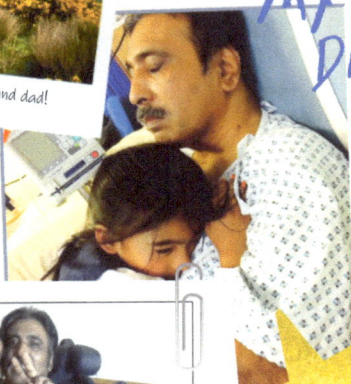

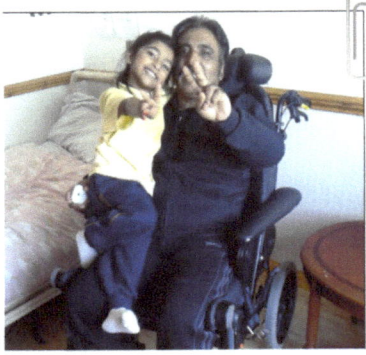

New home in Cork!

Dad's Restaurant, Wexford 2009

www.ingramcontent.com/pod-product-compliance
Lightning Source LLC
Chambersburg PA
CBHW060815090426
42737CB00002B/70